How to Drive Safely

49 Expert Tips, Tricks, and Advice for New, Teen Drivers

by Damian Brindle

===> Get dozens of free survival guides, hundreds of videos, 600+ "how to" articles, gear reviews and so much more here: https://rethinksurvival.com

Disclaimer

The material covered within is for informational purposes only. I take no responsibility for what you do with this knowledge and I cannot be held responsible for any property or medical damages caused by the items or information you read about within. I would advise you to check your local laws as it's possible that some of the items or advice I offer may be illegal in some areas, and I would highly advise you against their use in said areas. Moreover, by using any information or material found within, you assume all risks for the material covered. You agree to indemnify, hold harmless, and defend the author, Damian Brindle, from all claims and damages arising from the use, possession or consequences of the information covered. By taking and/or using any informational resources found within, you agree that you will use this information in a safe and legal manner, consistent with all applicable laws, safety rules, and good common sense. You further agree that you will take such steps as may be reasonably necessary or required by applicable law to keep any information out of the hands of minors as well as untrained and/or irresponsible individuals.

Table of Contents

Introduction

This book is intended to provide useful, actionable safe driving strategies as quickly as possible. As such, it's written to be fast to read and includes minimal images. Links are provided to referenced products should you want additional information or to purchase the product for your vehicle.

To make these safety tips easier to reference and grasp, you'll find a new tip introduced every page or two, with a few exceptions.

About Website Links

Realize, too, that this was originally written to be an electronic book only with many website links referenced throughout. Because this is a paperback book, however, referencing these links can be tedious if you had to type them into your web browser by hand. To make this easier on you, I have consolidated all referenced links into one page here: **https://rethinksurvival.com/books/driving-links.html**.

When new links are introduced, they will be referenced with superscripts which will then correspond to the appropriate URL on the above referenced website page. I've also included Bit.ly links for all YouTube videos to make them easier to reference while reading.

For completeness, all referenced links will also be included in Appendix B.

Grab Your Free 49-Point Safe Driving Checklist

Odds are that you won't remember everything discussed when you're done reading this book. To make your life easier I've created a free, easy-to-reference 49-point safe driving checklist which you can download that outlines everything discussed herein. You'll find a link to it here so that you can follow along if you like as well as at the end of this book in Appendix A, but please do read the entire book first.

Now, download your free, easy-to-reference safe driving checklist here.[1]

Prepare Yourself for Natural Disaster in Only 5 Minutes

Since you clearly understand the need for safety on the road, I want to share with you my unique **5 Minute Survival Blueprint** where you'll discover just how to keep your family safe and secure from disasters of all kinds in only 5 minutes a day, fast, easy, and inexpensively.[2]

More Books You'll Enjoy

If you liked what you read when finished, you can find more useful books I've written at rethinksurvival.com/kindle-books.[3]

This Book's Tone

As noted before, this book is written in a quick, simple, easy to read format. Hence, it is presented in a conversational form and not one that is intended to be grammatically correct. Getting you, as a new, teenage driver ready for the road is the sole focus of this book.

And My Thanks

I also want to thank those folks who took the time to review this book, to offer their own suggestions, and to correct my mistakes. You know who you are.

The Most Dangerous Driving Times, Days, and Situations

We'll start with understanding when it's most dangerous for teens or, really, anyone to be on the road. The expectation is that with this knowledge you'll choose to be even more aware of what's going on around you during these times and situations if they cannot be avoided.

Surprisingly, it's not always late nights that are the most dangerous times to be out on the road. Similarly, it's not always Friday or Saturday nights that are the most dangerous days either. We'll cover precisely when you need to be more aware and why.

Moreover, there are a few specific instances which are more dangerous for drivers than many people realize—particularly teenagers—specifically the first day of a snowstorm, downed power lines, and flooded roadways, to name a few situations. We'll discuss each of these in turn so you understand why they're so dangerous.

Let get to it.

Safety Tip # 1: The Most Dangerous Times of the Day to Drive Might Not Be When You Think

Most parents, me included, wrongly assume that late weekend nights are the most dangerous times for teens to drive. While they're up there on the list, according to a study conducted by AAA, the most dangerous times for teen drivers are weekdays between 3 pm and 5pm.[4]

Similarly, according to the National Highway Traffic Safety Administration (NHTSA), the most dangerous times for anyone to be on the road day-to-day is during the evening rush hour, typically between 3 pm and 7 pm, though the exact time frame varies depending on the source referenced. Regardless, data consistently shows that the evening rush hour is clearly the worst time to be on the road for all of us, most likely because everyone is tired and in a hurry to get home after a long, stressful day at work or school.

This isn't to say, of course, that other times of the day aren't also dangerous. For instance, the wee-morning hours of between 12 am and 4 am on Saturday (from being out on Friday night) tend to have twice as many road fatalities as weekdays due to more people being intoxicated behind the wheel. I'd suspect that the same can be said for the early-morning hours on Sunday too. In either case, it's not a good time to be out no matter what your friends say.

Safety Tip # 2: Driving at Dusk or Dawn Is Dangerous for Other Reasons

Driving at dusk or dawn can be quite dangerous as well, but not necessarily because people are tired. This article explains why: "Dusk and dawn are dangerous times to be behind the wheel. The road surface, pedestrians and other vehicles often are shrouded in shadow at these hours, but the sky still can be fairly bright. That contrast creates a problem — the light sky prevents drivers' eyes from adjusting to the dark road. Meanwhile, the setting or rising sun sometimes is directly in our eyes...other drivers might not yet have turned on their headlights...and we might be feeling drowsy."[5]

Similarly, I've seen times where other drivers haven't turned on their headlights after leaving a well-lit parking area, yet it was relatively dark out, enough that another driver might not see them. This is an accident waiting to happen since we instinctively rely another vehicle's headlights to see them coming. Please always remember to turn on your headlights if it's even close to still being dark out.

Again, it isn't just about what you, as the driver, are doing improperly, it's also very much about what other drivers are doing as well. As such, it's up to you to be even more cognizant of other drivers during these riskiest times of the day to be on the road.

Safety Tip # 3: The Most Dangerous Days of the Year to Drive May Also Surprise You

The summer months—specifically Memorial Day through Labor Day—are considered the 100 deadliest days for teen drivers, according to the NHTSA.

That said, a Snopes article suggests the rise in fatality rates during the summer may simply be because people are on the road during the summertime more often and for longer than other months. Thus, if we normalize for miles driven, those summer months might not be worse than any other month.[6]

Regardless, according to the same Snopes article, the Fourth of July continues to be one of the deadliest driving days and has been for decades now. It's followed closely by most other major holidays, including Christmastime, New Year's, Thanksgiving weekend, and most weekends in August. A more recent article lists Memorial Day as being the worst day to be on the road, followed by July 4th, Labor Day, and the other major holiday weekends.[7]

Clearly, all the major holidays, as well as the weekend days surrounding them tend to be the most dangerous driving days for everyone on the road. The summer months, however, tend to be more dangerous for teens, most likely due to alcohol consumption, though, distractions from their friends being in the car may be the biggest factor of them all.

Safety Tip # 4: Why the First Day of a Snowstorm Is Worst of All

Unfortunately, holidays and weekends aren't the only times to worry about being on the road, teenager or not. I've long contested that people forget how to drive in winter weather conditions after a long time without having done so, and this article backs me up, stating: "The first day of a snowstorm is dangerous for drivers. The whole cold season doesn't bring as many traffic collisions and fatalities as the first day of snowing. Fender-benders are 14% more likely to happen on the first day of snow than later in the snowy season."[8]

Of course, it's not merely teenagers who tend to drive poorly in the snow, experienced drivers do as well. It's not unheard of to see many vehicles stuck in a ditch on the highway, in particular, on the first day of a snowstorm simply because they failed to slow down.

As such, if you live anywhere that it tends to snow or the roads may ice up over the winter, I would strongly encourage you to ask your parents to take you out and to practice driving in these conditions, if you haven't had the chance yet. After all, it's one thing to explain that you need to slow down and quite another to truly experience it for yourself.

Safety Tip # 5: Why SUVs May Be More Dangerous Than Other Cars During the Winter

Taking NHTSA and the Insurance Institute for Highway Safety (IIHS) safety ratings of vehicles and tires out of the equation for a moment, SUVs are NOT any safer to drive during poor weather conditions than any other vehicle. That is, they cannot stop or turn better than any other vehicle in snowy or icy conditions simply because they're an SUV.

Not surprisingly, this article points out that, "During the non-winter months, SUVs make up about 16% of all crashes. But consistently, when winter arrives, that percentage moves up to 18%. That 2 percent matters when you're talking about a total of 50-60,000 winter crashes."[9]

I know two percent doesn't sound like much, but it is statistically significant enough to suggest that people do seem to believe SUVs are safer to drive in poor weather conditions, which inevitably causes them to drive at higher rates of speed than they otherwise would have thereby resulting in an easily avoidable accident if they had only slowed down.

On the other hand, there is something to be said for the fact that an SUV, or most any all-wheel drive or four-wheel drive vehicle, is more capable of getting moving in bad weather conditions than their two-wheel drive counterparts.

That is, SUVs are more likely to avoiding getting stuck in snow in the first place, partly due to factors such as a higher ground clearance and usually having more than one powered drive wheel. In addition, SUVs may sometimes be equipped with winter tires which do provide better traction during wintry conditions.

These factors combined will make SUVs more capable during poor wintertime conditions overall. They do not, regrettably, mean that a driver can ignore road conditions and drive as they wish.

For this reason, I would suggest that you as a new, teen driver learn from your parents how to drive in poor winter weather without the aid of—or perceived safety from—an SUV. In so doing, you'll understand how to respect road conditions first and, hopefully, will translate that respect to whatever vehicle you drive in the future.

Finally, if you do have an SUV you can use to practice with then you should understand how and when to use the four-wheel drive features of the vehicle if, for example, you have to manually shift into and out of four-wheel drive. Fortunately, many vehicles these days are equipped with all-wheel drive or full-time four-wheel drive features which means you don't have to do anything except drive. Even so, it's good to practice under the supervision of an experienced adult if you're unsure of what you're doing.

Safety Tip # 6: Any Inclement Weather Can Be Dangerous, Not Merely Snowy and Icy Roads

I don't want you to get the impression that only poor winter weather can make driving dangerous. There are absolutely many other instances where driving can become problematic for all of us on the road.

For example, periods of heavy rain may cause localized flooding which, when driven over at higher rates of speed, may cause a driver to hydroplane thus losing control of their vehicle. Here's a good video detailing what happens when a vehicle hydroplanes and what to do about it: https://bit.ly/2y5Bxnx.[10]

Again, nearly any inclement weather scenario can cause trouble for drivers, from dense fog or glaring sunlight making the roadway difficult to see, to high winds and severe storms making it difficult to even stay on the road at times, there's often something to be cautious of.

Aside from the obvious troubles that snow and ice cause, fog is one of the worst conditions because it doesn't quite feel like bad weather yet can obscure your vision to almost nothing at times. It's deceiving!

Ultimately, reducing one's speed considerably is usually the best course of action to prevent accidents from happening as a result of most any bad weather conditions.

Safety Tip # 7: Downed Power Lines Should NEVER Be Driven Over

This is true even if you think they're not still energized and, at the very least, lines can become entangled in your tires. If you would like more information, here's some good safety advice if you ever encounter downed power line, plus four interesting myths about power lines you should read, as well.[11, 12]

As you can see from the photo below, downed trees or tree branches are usually the biggest reason for power lines to come down. Clearly, this will make attempting to traverse such a hazard even more difficult and all the more reason not to even try.

Figure 1

Safety Tip # 8: Flooded Roads Should NEVER Be Driven Over Either

Even if only a foot or two of water seem to be covering the roadway, it's nothing to chance. This National Oceanic and Atmospheric (NOAA) article explains why:

"Each year, more deaths occur due to flooding than from any other thunderstorm related hazard. The Centers for Disease Control and Prevention report that over half of all flood-related drownings occur when a vehicle is driven into hazardous flood water. The next highest percentage of flood-related deaths is due to walking into or near flood waters. People underestimate the force and power of water. Many of the deaths occur in automobiles as they are swept downstream. Of these drownings, many are preventable, but too many people continue to drive around the barriers that warn you the road is flooded. A mere 6 inches of fast-moving flood water can knock over an adult. It takes just 12 inches of rushing water to carry away a small car, while 2 feet of rushing water can carry away most vehicles. It is NEVER safe to drive or walk into flood waters."[13]

Remember the slogan: Turn Around, Don't Drown!

I'd say that sums it up nicely but, just in case, flooded roads and vehicles do NOT mix and are the number one reason for drowning deaths during storms.

Floodwaters are powerful and never to be taken lightly. This is where the road ends for now.

Figure 2

My advice to all drivers when confronted with dangerous situations: When in doubt and clearly safe to do so, pull over until the threat passes or subsides enough for it to be safe to resume driving again or, at the very least, SLOW DOWN. And if you do pull over to the side of the road, ensure you're well away from traffic and that your headlights and hazards are on for safety. If still in doubt about driving on, ask yourself this: Would your grandmother feel safe riding in the car with you? If not, you're probably driving too fast for the weather conditions or even driving when you shouldn't be. Keep grandma happy.

Always Do This Before Driving Off

Now that you have an understanding as to which times, days, and situations are the most dangerous for all drivers, we need to get you situated in your vehicle properly.

That is, we're going to ensure that you, the driver, are as safe as you can be and, believe it or not, it starts before you even put your vehicle in gear.

None of this will take long, and if you drive the same car each day then most of these recommendations will have already been done. If, however, you share a vehicle or drive different vehicles then pay extra attention to this chapter so that you're not making adjustments while driving.

Here's what to do before you get moving.

Safety Tip # 9: Adjust Your Seat, Mirrors, and Everything Else Properly Before Driving Off

If you're driving an unfamiliar vehicle or you share a vehicle with others, odds are that some things need to be adjusted. Take a moment to ensure the driver's seat and steering wheel are correctly aligned, that both the rearview and sideview mirrors are positioned appropriately, and that the headrest is adjusted correctly because it's not just there for comfort, but for your rear-end accident safety too.

Seat Adjustment

I'm sure that as you get more comfortable driving you may be tempted to perform these adjustments on the fly because you're in a hurry. I know, I've done it myself, but things don't always go as expected. For instance, one time I adjusted my driver's seat after swapping spots with my wife on a long drive, but instead of the seat clicking into place as I expected, the seat moved all the way rearward, so much so that I could no longer reach the pedals! I had to unbuckle in order to readjust the seat and, while I was doing so, I inadvertently pulled the steering wheel and nearly got into an accident at 70 mph. Lesson learned.

Mirror Adjustments

Until recently, I'd always had my sideview mirrors pointing directly down the sides of my vehicle so that I could more easily backup, relying on both the rearview mirror and side mirrors to do so. In order to see driver's lurking in my blind spots, however, I always relied on those tiny blind spot mirrors and, as it turns out, I've been doing it wrong all along. You're supposed to have the side mirrors pointing quite far out away from your vehicle, so far, in fact, that they're no longer useful for reversing and, instead, truly cover your blind spots. To adjust side mirrors properly, place your face next to the driver's door window and adjust the left mirror until you can see down the side of your car again, then attempt to sit in or position yourself in the middle of the car and adjust the right mirror until you can see down the passenger side of the car. Here's a video on how to do so, if you need a visual: https://bit.ly/2RpBI41.[13b]

Adjusting Everything Else

Get everything else situated as well, especially the steering wheel and headrest, and make sure nothing is under your feet because things can roll around and get lodged under the pedals. You may need to adjust the A/C or heater too, maybe type in some GPS directions, who knows. Odds are that you have a smartphone too and will want to get some music playing or, at the very least, play music on the radio. Now's the time to get everything else squared away.

None of this should take more than 30 seconds to a minute at most in a new vehicle, and there's no reason to be doing any of it while you're driving.

Safety Tip # 10: Why You've Been Holding the Steering Wheel Wrong All Along

When I grew up, I was told to hold the steering wheel at 10 and 2 as if the steering wheel were a clock face. Truth be told, I still tend to hold the steering wheel like this. Perhaps you learned to do so as well.

The problem is that you and I may be holding the steering wheel wrong and it could be very costly. Why? Because of airbags, as this article points out:

"...Doing it the old way could risk serious injuries to a driver's hands or fingers if the airbag activates, as MSNBC recently reported: That means the higher up the wheel your hands are, the more likely they are to be directly over the plastic cover when it opens... when superhot nitrogen gas flashes and inflates the bag at 150 to 250 mph. Among the injuries the NHTSA reports from improper placement of the hands when an airbag deploys are amputations of fingers or entire hands, traumatic fractures and a particularly stomach-churning injury called 'degloving,' which — trust us — you definitely don't want to look up."[14]

While that sounds horrible enough, it gets worse. According to my cousin, who is a longtime police officer, there's also the possibility of your hands being flung into your face at a high rate of impact when the airbag deploys thereby doing even more damage to your face than the airbag alone could have.

And if you think that holding the steering wheel at the 12 o'clock position is any better, it's not. From now on I'm going to start holding the steering wheel at the 9 and 3 position as the authorities recommend since that appears to be the safest option of all. I suggest you do as well.

What About Other Airbags in the Vehicle?

Most newer vehicles have passenger-side airbags and even side-impact airbags too. But, as you now understand, they can do considerable damage to occupants which is why there are age and weight restrictions for the front passenger seat if there's an airbag present. Therefore, if you're going to be driving young siblings around who don't meet the front seat age or weight requirements, please ensure they sit in the backseat for safety from both the impact of a collision as well as the force of an airbag deployment.

Never Rely on Airbags Alone

You're almost always better off being properly restrained with a seat belt inside of your vehicle than being ejected from it no matter what you may have heard anecdotally, such as from friends. Even if you aren't flung out of the vehicle because of not wearing a seat belt, please don't think an airbag alone will save you because it's only intended as a supplemental restraint, not the primary one, and for good reason.

Safety Tip # 11: Use Seat Belts, They Really Do Save Many Thousands of Lives Each Year

The statistics overwhelmingly prove that seat belts save lives. In fact, a CDC factsheet states:

- More than half (range: 52%-59%) of teens (13-19 years) and adults aged 20-44 years who died in crashes in 2015 were unrestrained at the time of the crash.
- Young adult drivers and passengers (18-24) have the highest crash-related non-fatal injury rates of all adults.[15]

The numbers are undeniable. While increasingly people do wear seat belts regularly, a good percentage still don't. Besides, it's against the law in every state for anyone under eighteen years of age not to wear them and often a secondary offense in most states if you're over the age of eighteen and pulled over while not wearing one.

I realize numbers don't always get the attention they warrant. For that reason, here's a few videos to consider watching that may hammer the point home:

- Consequences of Driving Without a Seat Belt: https://bit.ly/2RmEfvW.[16]
- Crash Test With and Without Safety Belt: https://bit.ly/2RorLnl.[17]
- No Seat Belt Crashes: https://bit.ly/3ecCxan.[18]

Safety Tip # 12: Turn on Headlights for Safety

I would encourage you to turn on your headlights if it's not plainly daytime and sunny out. Truth be told, it's probably a good habit to practice no matter what since having your headlights on almost never hurts, even in broad daylight. Realize that some vehicles are equipped with daytime running lights, and if your vehicle is then this advice isn't necessary. Otherwise, you should read on.

For starters, weather conditions can change in the blink of an eye. For example, it was sunny out when you left the house, but now it's cloudy or raining and quite a bit darker too. In this situation, turning your lights on may be a good decision, but what if you forgot to turn them on when the weather changed? If you had your lights on in the first place, then there's no need to worry. Beyond that, some states require you to have your headlights on if you also have your windshield wipers on, as well as for a variety of other reasons.[19] Honestly, I was a bit surprised at how differing individual state laws were regarding headlight usage during the daytime, which could be one more good reason to simply keep them on.

As stated before, the environment may make things difficult to see. For example, you're driving along a roadway where a line of trees allows sunlight to occasionally filter through, yet the constant back and forth of sunlight versus no sunlight is very distracting.

Having your headlights on, in this case, may be just enough for other drivers to see you coming when they otherwise may not have. Remember, headlights aren't just about you being able to see the road, but also about other's being able to see YOU as well.

Figure 3

And, as you might suspect, studies show that having your lights on during the day can decrease accidents by 5 to 10 percent, according to this lengthy report.[20]

While your vehicle should alert you if you left your lights on when you turn the engine off, it might not if there's a problem. I had a car that didn't alert me if I left the lights were left on because of a simple door switch malfunction, and I can attest that I've returned to more than one dead battery as a result. Have it repaired so you don't encounter the same situation.

Not Speeding is Much More Than Avoiding Tickets

I'm sure most experienced drivers would agree that speeding is something we've all done and, for some people, still do. Sometimes the speed limit slips our mind because we're thinking about something else, or perhaps that lead foot kicks in without realizing it, or we're plain in a hurry and know we're speeding. I get the reasons, but they really don't matter because speeding is a major contributing factor to accidents, and it's entirely preventable.

In fact, a recent NHTSA Safety Facts sheet clearly shows that speeding is a contributing factor in 30% or more of traffic accidents year after year.[21]

Remember that speeding isn't just about exceeding the posted speed limit, but also about driving too fast for the road conditions. That's why it's possible for a police officer to write you a speeding ticket even if you're driving at the posted speed limit; he or she has determined that you're driving too fast to be safe, such as in very icy or foggy conditions, and you should have known to slow down.

But there's more to speeding, in particular, with regards to teenage drivers.

Safety Tip # 13: Age and Alcohol Consumption Increase Speeding Rates and Fatalities

Although many factors can play a part, such as friends being in the vehicle or being distracted by a text message you've been waiting for, there are two major contributing factors related to being a teenage driver and the likelihood of speeding which stand out above them all: relative age and alcohol use. Let's discuss these one at a time.

Factor 1: Age (and gender to a lesser degree)

Age is a huge factor with regards to speeding and driving fatalities as the above-referenced NHTSA Safety Facts sheet states: "For drivers involved in fatal crashes, young males are the most likely to be speeding... In 2012, 24 percent of female drivers in the 15- to 20-year-old age group and 19 percent of female drivers in the 21- to 24-year-old age group involved in fatal crashes were speeding at the time of the crash. Among males, 37 percent of 15- to 20-year-old and 37 percent of 21- to 24-year-old drivers involved in fatal crashes were speeding."[21]

I can say that, as a teenager and surely as a young adult, I've had my fair share of speeding tickets. Over time I've learned the hard way that it wasn't worth the price I paid in traffic fines and court fees or, worse, the risk of causing a bad accident happening.

Factor 2: Alcohol makes things far worse

I'll assume that at age twenty-one you probably have a few years of driving experience under your belt. This is both a blessing and curse because it means that you're not only a more capable driver, but also comfortable enough to take risks since driving is now second nature to you. Sadly, one of the risks many young people choose to take is drinking and driving.

Alcohol consumption tends to cause even more serious trouble than a lack of experience driving as the aforementioned fact sheet goes on to say: "In 2012, 28 percent of the speeding drivers under age 21 who were involved in fatal crashes also had BACs of .08 g/dL or higher. In contrast, only 13 percent of the non-speeding drivers under 21 involved in fatal crashes in 2012 had BACs of .08 g/ dL or higher. For drivers 21 to 24 years old who were involved in fatal crashes in 2012, 50 percent of speeding drivers had BACs of .08 g/dL or higher, compared with only 24 percent of non-speeding drivers."[21]

Those statistics are nothing to be taken lightly as they more than double your chances of a fatal car accident. It just doesn't pay to drink and drive no matter how unintoxicated you think you are or what your friends say. The same can be said for use of drugs, like marijuana. Enlist a designated driver or, better yet, be the designated driver. Everyone will thank you.

Safety Tip # 14: Speeding Doesn't Actually Save You Time in Almost Any Scenario

Like I said, I've had my fair share of speeding tickets when I was younger, and I know people who have accumulated many multiples more than I have. As I've aged, I understand now how pointless it is to speed and, consequently, have tended to slow down so much so that family accuse me of driving like a grandpa already. Alas, many folks don't see it the same way as I do, even as adults.

Truth be told, speeding really doesn't help you save much time at all which most of us intuitive know, yet tend to ignore. To make my point, I found an interesting article which breaks down just how much time is theoretically saved at different speeds and distances traveled. The takeaway is that you might save at most a few minutes on trips under an hour and, as the article points out, "...the higher the speed limit is already, the less time you save by exceeding it, not more."[22]

When you factor in speeding on city streets where congestion and traffic lights slow down your progress substantially, the odds are that you won't save much, if any, time whatsoever. The article concludes with a mind-blowing reality-check, stating: "To put all these savings of a few minutes into perspective, let's assume the average speeding ticket cost is $150. In order for six minutes [the assumed time savings from a hypothetical trip] of your time to be worth $150, you would have to make $1,500/hour or about $3,000,000 per year."[22]

In my experience, that assumed $150 per ticket is a low estimate, especially when you realize that (1) the more over the speed limit you are the larger the fine will be with teens tending to have higher rates of speed and (2) the states where you're most likely to receive a ticket also impose the highest fines. Factor in that some states let you fix a ticket by paying a lawyer to make it a nonmoving violation and, thus, avoid points on your license, you'll pay even more.

About the only time that speeding appears to save any significant amount of time is on a very long road trip of hundreds of miles or more which is precisely when mild speeding of, say, under ten mile per hour, helps least all things considered.

That said, I don't want you to take any of this as a reason to speed at any time or over any distance traveled. I imagine you still will at times, surely by mistake if nothing else, but I can attest that it's simply not worth the risk to either your wallet or your safety. If you're finding yourself having to speed because you're running late all the time, get out of the door sooner. I promise you'll be happier you did and less stressed out on the road as well.

Safety Tip # 15: Teens Are Far More Likely to Be Targeted for Speeding Than All Other Ages

You might be interested in reading a study titled, *Who Gets Speeding Tickets and Why?,* conducted in Minnesota if you simply must know the precise factors authorities tend to consider most when giving out tickets. Besides miles per hour over the speed limit and time of day, age plays a big role here too.

The article states: "Age is a huge factor in who gets ticketed. The younger people are way more likely to get ticketed for speeding and the officers who spoke to this said that it is a clear fact: Young drivers tend to drive faster than older drivers. Those in the 16 – 25-year-old demographic got one third of all speeding tickets in the study. While drivers 40 and over got another third, the two groups are very different in size. The younger group makes up less than 15 percent of the state's population while the older group is just about half the state. Clearly, the younger group is being ticketed at a much higher rate and law enforcement says that it is deserved. When graphed by age, there is a huge decline in tickets after the age of 19. And this holds true for both male and female drivers."[23]

Deservedly so or not, teenage drivers are targeted more for speeding than all other age groups, and you'll have a target on your back for years to come.

Safety Tip # 16: Slowing Down Even Slightly Makes a Big Difference in Accident Prevention

I found this interesting example of how only five miles an hour difference can not only dramatically change the likelihood of an accident, but even possibly result in a wrongful death lawsuit: "A pedestrian walks out into a crosswalk with an approaching car that is traveling at 30 mph. If the driver brakes when the pedestrian is 45 feet away, there will be enough space to stop without hitting the pedestrian. Now, increase the vehicle's speed by just 5 mph, and the situation changes dramatically. At 35 mph and the pedestrian 45 feet away, the car will be traveling at 18 mph when it hits the pedestrian. A pedestrian accident at 18 mph can cause major injuries or even wrongful death."[24]

While an interesting hypothetical, there are surely a few factors involved in how quickly a vehicle will come to a stop, including vehicle weight, braking capabilities, road surface conditions, and reaction speed, to name a few. The point is that even a slight reduction in speed can dramatically alter an outcome, often more so than most people realize, and not just when pedestrians are involved.

Car accidents are nothing to be taken lightly. They can be costly when insurance gets involved and may cause serious injury, even at seemingly low speeds.

Safety Tip # 17: The Three-Second Trick for Preventing Car Accidents at ANY Speed

The same website referenced in the previous safety tip discusses the three second rule for preventing car accidents at any speed. Basically, you watch for the vehicle ahead of you to pass by a static object such as a light pole and count for three seconds. If you get to the object you picked out before you can count to three, you're too close. Of course, this assumes a dry, straight roadway. If the road conditions are poor or you're driving at highways speeds, then you'll need to double the time. And if the roads are icy or snowy then add a few more seconds.

Another way that I've heard to check if your trailing distance is too close is this: if you can read the license plate of the vehicle in front of you then you're too close. Personally, I don't use this method.

The rule of thumb that I grew up with is to allow at least ten feet of distance for every ten miles per hour in speed. For example, if you're driving at twenty miles per hour you would leave twenty feet of distance between your vehicle and the one you're following, fifty miles per hour would need at least fifty feet of distance, and so on. Double that distance in rain or other inclement weather. Remember, this is the bare minimum safe distance to allow when following a vehicle. It never hurts to allow for more.

Don't Do Any of This While Driving

I'll be honest, the older we drivers get the more accustomed to driving we become and, therefore, the more willing we may be to perform potentially unsafe actions while behind the wheel.

This could include many activities, from adjusting the radio or eating to applying makeup or helping out kids in the backseat, and who knows what else.

I know I've done plenty of things I probably shouldn't have over the years, and I've seen many people do things while on the road that they certainly shouldn't have been doing either.

It feels almost inevitable.

Let's just be realistic about what you can and should do while driving, which brings me to the most important action to avoid above all others: interacting with your smartphone.

If you, as a new driver, fully understand just how crucial it is to leave your smartphone alone while driving, you'll be well ahead of nearly all of your peers and you'll be that much safer as a result.

Safety Tip # 18: Smartphones Are the Biggest Distraction Ever, Leave Them Be When Driving

Distracted driving is nothing to overlook. Anything that takes your focus away from the road is a distraction, though, not all distractions are equal. For instance, it's one thing to quickly change the car radio station to another preset, yet quite another to search for a new song on your smartphone. And trying to read or, worse, respond to a text message is just asking for trouble. Now, because smartphones are such a huge concern, we're going to spend more than the typical page or two discussing them.

Smartphones are the number one distraction while driving these days, particularly for teen drivers. As a matter of fact, this article states that: "Research has found that dialing a phone number while driving increases your teen's risk of crashing by six times, and texting while driving increases the risk by 23 times. Talking or texting on the phone takes your teen's focus off the task of driving, and significantly reduces their ability to react to a roadway hazard, incident, or inclement weather."[25]

While it's not just teens who are so distracted by their phones, they are the most likely group to feel a need to be always on their phones, even in the car. As such, you're probably going to have to do something different while driving.

Figure 4

I've seen from my own experience how distracting smartphones can be and, more importantly, how easy it is to completely lose focus on the road when trying to use a phone in the car. I've witnessed numerous instances where people have been driving quite erratically on the road during broad daylight, only to later see that they had their head buried in a phone, most likely trying to read and respond to a text message or social media thread.

Furthermore, a recent study points out that: "...in 52 percent of all wrecks, drivers had been on their phones. These aren't just fender benders – 29 percent of drivers were doing over 56 miles per hour... Texting, browsing social media and email are the most common distractions. The average duration of distraction was 135 seconds."[26]

What I find most interesting about that statement is the "average duration of distraction was 135 seconds" and, to be honest, I have no idea how that's even possible. Even a few seconds of my attention being taken away because I was staring at my phone is enough for me to lose focus on the road. I've learned from experience to leave my phone alone in the car whenever I'm moving.

I can't say that I haven't had extra incentive. In Washington state, where I live, they passed a ban on using phones while driving in 2017. At first, I wasn't very happy about yet another roadway law to obey, particularly one that told me I couldn't do something which I had been doing for a long time, that is, talking on my phone in the car. But I do understand the reasoning behind the push to limit phone usage in the car and, so, I've taken it to heart and generally agree with the law these days.

Even if your state doesn't outright ban phone usage in the car, you should ban phone usage yourself. In my experience, I've noticed that since we've allowed our oldest son to have a phone, he's on it all the time, even in the car. Knowing that he was going to start driving on his own soon, I began to make him get off his phone while we're driving in preparation for him getting behind the wheel because I can see that he's associated being in the car with being on his phone. I had even gone so far as to not begin driving until he's finished with the latest, most crucial Instagram or text comment he "Just has to do really quick, Dad!"

Now that he's been driving for more than a year on his own, he seems to have understood the need to stay off his phone while driving, at least, he says he doesn't do any texting or anything highly distracting like that. Hopefully, he will continue to be smart about it and I would encourage you to be as well.

Sadly, even this attempted change in behavior won't be enough for many teens. We really must look to technology to help combat smartphone usage while in the car because, to be frank, most teens will completely ignore parental advice when it comes to interacting with the world, especially when parents are not around. Therefore, if you feel you won't be able to leave your phone alone while driving then I would suggest you download and install a safe driving smartphone app to help you get into the habit. On a positive note, many insurance companies are rewarding you with discounts for staying off your phone and there are now apps, such as OnMyWay, which pays you to not use your phone while driving.[26b] I suspect there will be more apps like this coming in the near future.

Safety Tip # 19: Don't Wear Earbuds or Headsets While Driving and Avoid Loud Music

Another thing I've noticed young driver's doing is wearing earbuds or even entire headsets while driving. This isn't very safe, especially when both ears are covered because you're far less able to hear emergency vehicle sirens, honking horns, screeching tires, and who knows what else. Furthermore, when the windows are closed and music is playing it's hard to hear anything going on outside, even more so if you're also wearing earbuds or a headset.

That said, I do realize they make Bluetooth earbuds for use with a phone while driving. If you're going to use them for this purpose, just be sure to not cover both ears so you can still hear something going on outside. Surprisingly, most states do not have restrictions on wearing headsets while driving, here's a reference if you're curious.[27]

Playing loud music is another concern I should briefly mention as it's something many teenagers do—including my son—and possibly something you'll do as well. I really don't imagine he can hear much of anything going on outside unless it's right on top of him and neither will you if the music is blaring. Do yourself a favor and try not to play music at maximum volume. You'll save your hearing down the road and maybe avoid an accident in the meantime.

Safety Tip # 20: Never Tailgate, Especially at Highway Speeds

Driving extremely closely to the vehicle in front of you, also known as tailgating, is another big cause of preventable automobile accidents at any speed, though in my opinion, clearly worse at higher speeds. Even if in bumper to bumper traffic, you should, at the very least, be able to see the rear tires of the vehicle in front of you and, as was mentioned previously, ideally NOT be able to read their license plate. Granted, if you're in the thick traffic you probably won't be able to give yourself that much distance or else people will be constantly sneaking in front of you.

Realize, however, that tailgating is different than simply following a bit too closely. It's taking a potentially dangerous situation (that of being too close to begin with) to an extreme by creating an obviously dangerous situation for everyone nearby, and likely stressing out the driver in front of you who could then do something wrong and make it worse.

Most of us intuitively know if we're driving too closely, and tailgating is a no-brainer. Often, we're in a hurry or being tailed by an impatient driver ourselves which, in turn, causes us to drive closer than is safe. If you realize you're too close, do the right thing and back off a bit. If needed, pull over when safe to do so and let the impatient drivers pass.

Safety Tip # 21: Stop Trying to Make Yellow Lights and NEVER Run Red Lights

Another easily preventable situation is that of running yellow or red lights. Running red lights will surely increase the chances of a side-impact collision which you could be prosecuted and sued for. Plus, trying to beat yellow lights probably means you're speeding, which we've already shown is pointless.

I see people run lights often enough and I've done it myself because I was in a hurry. No doubt, you will eventually run a stoplight as well. According to this PDF article, running red lights could be the most dangerous driving mistake of them all: "A crash caused by a driver who runs a red light is more likely to result in serious injury or death. Deaths caused by red-light running are increasing at more than three times the rate of increase for all other fatal crashes. More people are injured in crashes involving red-light running than in any other crash type.... [and that] Most people run red lights because they are in a hurry, when in fact they save only seconds."[28]

One part of the previous statement is absolutely something to reiterate here, so I will: "Deaths caused by red-light running are increasing at more than three times the rate of increase for all other fatal crashes. More people are injured in crashes involving red-light running than in any other crash type."[28]

Sure, if you beat the light you won't have to wait another minute or two for it to turn green again. I get it. But a lifetime of living in a wheelchair because your spine was crushed beyond repair, or you severely injured someone else such as a younger sibling or, worse, caused a death, is never worth saving a few minutes of time.

You should remember this the next time you're in a hurry and consider running a stoplight. The same can be said for stop signs. Even though you're likely travelling at a lower rate of speed than at a signal light, the odds of encountering a pedestrian or bicyclist near a stop sign, for example, are much greater and, thus, the likelihood of very serious injury to them is that much greater as well. Very shortly thereafter, lawyers and insurance companies will make your life extremely miserable for a long time.

Remember, too, that it's not just about YOU running a stoplight, it's also about cross-traffic drivers doing so as well. Therefore, if you're one of the first few drivers waiting at a stoplight, give a quick glance both ways with your peripheral vision just to be sure that a car isn't about to come barreling through the intersection as you get moving again yourself. Although there is usually a built-in delay at signal lights, they're not foolproof.

Safety Tip # 22: Railroad Crossing Continue to Be Deadly, Just Wait for the Train to Cross

Did you know that there are thousands of collisions and hundreds of fatalities every year because of vehicles becoming stranded at a railroad crossing or, more likely, motorists trying to beat a speeding train before it gets there? Luckily, these numbers have been steadily declining over the years, but there's no reason why they shouldn't be at zero every year.

Although your car is designed to help you survive most vehicular collisions, the truth is that most of the vehicle body is lightweight sheet metal, even plastic, particularly the sides of the vehicle where a collision is most likely to occur with a train. Your car simply doesn't stand a chance when that much force is involved because it was never designed to. In the case of your car versus a train, the train ALWAYS wins.[29]

If interested, you can easily find videos online of some very serious collisions between trains and motor vehicles of all types, including very large semi-trucks that didn't stand a chance despite their much larger mass than a typical motor vehicle. If interested, this video is a compilation of train versus vehicle collisions and, although a bit graphic, should help you to realize just how much of an unstoppable force a loaded freight train truly is and why you should avoid them at all costs: https://bit.ly/2RnjrV3.[29b]

Communicate With Other Drivers Properly and Respectfully

Understanding when and, perhaps more importantly, when not to use your vehicle to communicate with others driver's is a skill that you'll hone over time.

That said, it's important for you to have a solid basis as to how and why you should or shouldn't, for instance, use your high beams to signal other drivers. Do it right and they'll appreciate your doing so; do it wrong and you could cause an accident.

The same can be said for knowing how and when to signal with your brakes (yes, it's more than only signaling that you're coming to a stop) as well as when to use your horn and even your turn signals.

You might be surprised at how often even seasoned driver's get these things wrong.

Safety Tip # 23: Use Your Blinkers to Signal Turns, Lane Changes, and More

This may seem obvious, but oftentimes people get lazy and don't bother to signal their intentions. Most of the time this isn't a problem because other drivers can usually see what's going on and it's obvious that a vehicle is going to turn right, for example.

Remember that we're making assumptions about other drivers—and they about you—all the time and, so, if you do something they don't expect no matter whether you signaled or not then you could wind up in an accident that was your fault.

I know I'm not perfect, and I don't expect you to be all the time either, but I do try to signal my intentions whenever there's another vehicle around me, not just behind me, and well before I make my move so there's no confusion about what I'm intending. After all, it's not only the courteous thing to do, but the law in every state. This article states that: "...it's illegal if you do not signal your intentions before maneuvers. You are legally required to signal before pulling over, pulling into traffic, lane changing, parking, merging, turning right and left, etc. And yes, you can get a ticket for failing to signal your intentions."[30]

Basically, anytime you intend to do something other than continue straight down the lane you're driving in, you should be using your blinkers to signal others.

45

Safety Tip # 24: Use Brake Lights to Signal Slow Downs and Hazard Lights for Odd Stops

Tap your brake lights early on if you see traffic slowing down up ahead to signal driver's behind you that you may be braking soon, especially if you're driving a large vehicle that makes it difficult to see over or around you. This advice is particularly true for highway driving, as doing so could save your life. I won't get into details, but my in-laws were involved in a very serious highway accident about a decade ago because of a similar situation. They almost died and their lives have never been the same since.

Regarding hazard lights: There are times where you might end up not quite on the road and not fully parked, or maybe you just stopped next to the grocery store curb to let someone out. In situations like these, it's wise to let others know that you're clearly stopped by flashing your hazard lights.

Of course, I don't want to suggest that you're doing the right thing in the eyes of the law. You could very easily be stopped in a no parking zone which means that if somebody rear-ends you while you're parked there, even if only for a few seconds, that you're legally responsible even though you had your hazard lights on. But, if you're going to do what we all seem to do at some point, be as safe as possible and flash your hazard lights to warn others.

Safety Tip # 25: Use Your High Beam Lights Appropriately

Using your high beam lights are a big help at night when you're driving on roads without many streetlights or few drivers, such as on rural roads. I use mine on occasion, but there are times when I surely don't. For example, using high beam lights in the fog is usually a bad idea because they literally point at a higher angle than your low beam headlights which tends to illuminate the fog even more, thus making the road and street lines even more difficult to see. Rain and snow tend to make high beams less effective too.

Regarding high beam lights from oncoming traffic: Looking at an oncoming vehicle's high beam lights can be quite disorienting, especially if the weather is bad and you're already having trouble properly seeing the road. Of course, this largely depends on the relative height of each vehicle, that is, if the oncoming vehicle is a tall truck and you're driving a small sedan then their bright lights will be that much more in your eyes. Simply let them know they've got their high beams on by quickly flashing yours. If they don't turn off their bright lights, then you should keep your eyes focused on the right shoulder and the white line as a guide while you pass by. If it's the driver behind you who has their high beams on, the rearview mirror usually has an adjustment to counteract that problem.

Safety Tip # 26: When (And When NOT) to Use Your Car Horn

I remember watching a film in driver's education class decades ago where this instructor was showing you how to use your vehicle's horn to communicate with other drivers but, the thing was, he honked at everyone and for so many reasons. I can only image what driving would be like if everyone took his advice. Perhaps that's what driving in a big city, such as New York, is like? Yes, your car horn is there to communicate, but please use it wisely and sparingly.

Generally, you only want to use your car horn to avoid a possible collision because another driver is moving in such a way that they cannot see you approaching. With that in mind, don't use your horn to get somebody to speed up or move out of the way, because they made a mistake, or because you're upset about it and you want to let the other driver know how much. You also don't want to use your horn near a bicyclist or pedestrian unless they're doing something clearly wrong that may cause them to get injured.

Remember that your car horn is another useful communication tool, just as your brake lights and headlights are, but don't go overboard with using it or even fail to use your horn when obviously necessary.

More Commonsense Safety Tips to Know

By now you've got yourself properly situated in the car before driving off, you're leaving your smartphone alone, and you know how to communicate properly with other drivers.

What else could there be, you ask?

If you truly want to stay safe as much as possible while driving then there's plenty more to know, specifically these additional safety tips covering a wide range of topics, from medications and feeling tired to emergency vehicles and road rage.

We'll start with what's arguably the most important commonsense tip to abide by of them all: giving yourself extra time to get to where you're going.

It's something mostly of fail to do, particularly teenagers.

Safety Tip # 27: Give Yourself Five or Ten Extra Minutes to Get to Where You're Going

I know most of us are always in a hurry and, for some, this advice just won't work, but one of the best decisions you can make each day is to allow yourself an extra five or ten minutes to get to where you're going. Because, if this isn't clear already, being in a hurry is a primary cause of accidents happen.

If you willfully give yourself that extra bit of time then you won't be in such a hurry and, as a result, will be less likely to make a poor decision because you're running late and simply must get somewhere on time!

For example, we live near a relatively busy two-lane highway that's rather difficult to get onto since there's no traffic light. As a result, we often find ourselves having to wait for quite some time even, Heaven-forbid, entire minutes until there's a gap. When I'm rushed, I tend to take greater chances crossing and I'm sure others do as well. When I'm not in a hurry, I'll just wait.

Besides, being in a rush also means you're more likely to speed which is a huge contributing factor to accidents as we've covered previously. My advice, which my son has yet to appreciate: Set your alarm five or ten minutes earlier than normal and get out of the door that much sooner. You'll be happier that you're not in a rush and safer on the road as well.

Safety Tip # 28: Give Pedestrians, Bicyclists, and Motorcyclists Special Consideration

Pedestrians don't always have the legal right of way as is the case with jaywalking, but they do at intersections and crosswalks, for sure. Besides, there's no reason to hurt somebody or get into legal trouble because a pedestrian may not technically have the right of way at that moment. Always yield to pedestrians where possible. In addition, parking lots should be given special attention because most people never look for oncoming cars in lots anymore.

Occasionally, you'll encounter a bicyclist or, worse, a motorcyclist who is doing something wrong and causing you a problem. Realize that they're every bit as vulnerable as a pedestrian in a car accident, so please give them plenty of space as well.

Be aware that even bicyclists are required to follow local traffic laws. Thus, you may find them riding into the left-hand turn lane, signaling their intentions or turns with arm movements, and even riding into traffic if there's no bicycle lane available.

Last, the solid lines at intersections mean something, notably the crosswalks. Do you best not to infringe upon them so that pedestrians remain safe, but also so that you're less likely to be run into if, for example, a vehicle cuts the left turn short. You may end up being at fault.

Safety Tip # 29: If You're Feeling Tired, Pull Over and Rest

Usually about an hour into a long drive I start to feel sleepy. The feeling usually passes and I'm wide awake again for hours, but this is something I'm cognizant of, so I usually find a way to entertain myself until the feeling passes. When I've taken long trips on my own in the past of several hours or more, there is an inherent danger of getting tired and falling asleep at the wheel which, as I get older, I tend to avoid doing in order to avoid getting sleepy at the wheel.

The point is that if you're feeling tired, pull over where it's safe to do so. Get out, stretch your legs, grab a bite to eat, and swap drivers, if possible. Grab a hotel room if you must. We've done just that in the past. There's no reason to push it and end up in a devastating car accident.

Young drivers, in particular, may have additional reasons for feeling tired, including late-night study sessions, sports or other activities, part-time jobs, and more. You may be busier than ever before and may not even realize just how tired you are, even in the morning. Please realize how important it is to be mentally aware while driving and that if you ever do feel too tired to drive that you shouldn't do so and to ask for help.

Safety Tip # 30: Medications May REALLY Cause Drowsiness

As we discussed, the possibility of falling asleep at the wheel is no joke and can happen for reasons beyond merely feeling tired or because you stayed up too late. Medical conditions and medications are another primary culprit many people don't fully anticipate.

For instance, we have a close family friend who passed out at the wheel years ago due to a diabetic blood sugar crash and subsequently ran headlong into a tree. She's suffered severely ever since and likely won't ever be fully functional again, and all because of a momentary lapse in consciousness at the wheel due to a medical condition.

Medication use could be another reason for drowsiness. After all, many pharmaceuticals, even over-the-counter choices, often have warning labels which state they may cause drowsiness.

Similarly, drug interactions may cause drowsiness too. Therefore, it's imperative you never operate a motor vehicle until you know how new medications or changes to your medications affect your mental awareness. You really do need to consult a doctor or pharmacist if you're having any troubles with new medications so that you remain safe on the road. Here's a good reference about medications and driving safety should you need it.[31]

Safety Tip # 31: Avoid Late Night Driving, If Possible

For most teens, the setting sun means it's time to venture out and have some fun with friends. I know that's how I used to do it, often staying out into the wee hours of the morning for no good reason whatsoever. These days if it's close to nine or ten at night I'm looking for my pillow and the light switch.

Be aware that driving at night puts you at risk for an accident about threefold over the daytime average: "Car accident statistics are jarring at night. Despite 60 percent less traffic on the roads, more than 40 percent of all fatal car accidents occur at night."[32]

There's clearly a reason for such a massive difference in daytime versus nighttime accident statistics. Intoxicated drivers as well as the aforementioned drowsy drivers are more likely to be out on the road at night which clearly puts you at risk as well. Remember, too, that these aren't simple fender-benders, they're fatal accidents. I'm sure the statistics only get worse the later it gets.

I've told my son many times that nothing good ever happens after midnight. It's when people are coming home from the bars, when bad people are out looking for trouble, and when the cops are out searching too. Do yourself and your parents a favor and be home earlier, if possible.

Safety Tip # 32: Road Signs and Roadway Markings Are Trying to Tell You Something

I remember when I was much younger, I was driving downtown in an unfamiliar area, waiting patiently in stopped traffic, when I noticed a bunch of honking. To my surprise, people were honking at me! As it turns out, I was trying to make a left turn onto a one-way street. Others realized this since I had my blinker on. Fortunately, they got my attention, I realized my mistake, and I didn't make things worse. The problem, however, was that I didn't pay any attention to the signs that clearly stated the obvious. And, no, I wasn't distracted by my phone as this was before the time of smartphones, though I was probably lost in thought.

Solid-Yellow Lines Deserve a Special Mention

One very poor choice I occasionally see people make is that of choosing to pass slower vehicles on two-lane roads when there are obvious solid yellow lines indicating not to attempt to pass. Granted, sometimes these yellow-lines may feel a bit overcautious even though they're not, but there are clearly times where one shouldn't attempt to pass another vehicle, and these solid-yellow lines are trying to say just that.

Figure 5

Blind turns such as that depicted above as well as large dips or rises over hills are the biggest concerns here because you can't see what's on the other side of them. Personally, I've seen some very daring passing attempts over the years. Regrettably, I'm sure some daring passing attempts don't end well. After all, you're just asking for a high-speed, head-on collision if you or the other driver guess wrong, which is all the more reason to be extra cautious here.

The thing is that there often multiple signs and many painted markings on roadways that tell your precisely what you can and cannot do. Pay attention to them because they're trying to keep you safe. As always, attempting to save a few extra minutes time is never worth the risk.

Safety Tip # 33: Move Over for Emergency and Stopped Vehicle

I can't tell you how many times I've seen drivers— even on the highway—NOT move over for a stopped vehicle whether because of a breakdown, accident, or someone having been pulled over by an officer. Be a kind driver and move over a lane, if possible.

If you're ever in the same situation you'll appreciate the extra space because, as I can attest, there's no feeling quite like standing on the side of the highway trying to change a flat tire with vehicles flying by you at 70 mph or faster. I've heard of more than one death over the years because of situations like this.

Similarly, if there's an emergency vehicle wanting to get by you with the lights on, it's most assuredly trying to get somewhere in a hurry. Even if they must drive into the oncoming traffic lanes to get by you, they will, but get out of their way if you can do so safely. This scenario, happily, is something that most people get right. Just pull over to the right and wait for them to pass.

After all, one day it could be YOU out there on the side of the road with cars whizzing by while you're changing a tire or, worse, the person hoping that ambulance gets there just a bit faster.

Safety Tip # 34: Road Rage Is Truly Scary Stuff

I'm sure you've heard the term before. Maybe you've even experienced road rage, though, I hope not. Just to be clear, road rage is different from aggressive driving. This article explains the difference: "Aggressive driving is anything you do while driving that doesn't follow the law. It doesn't cause direct harm to another person or vehicle, though. A few examples include excessive speeding, tailgating, and giving hand gestures to other drivers. There is no physical harm to a person or vehicle, but the driving is still erratic and dangerous. In terms of the law, aggressive driving is a traffic violation. Road rage is a criminal offense."[33]

Basically, road rage is taking aggression too far and, according to the same article cited above, "80% of drivers admit to having some type of road rage during the course of a year... [and] at least 8 million drivers engage in some type of road rage each year."[33]

Moreover, this article reveals that: "More recent data from the National Highway Traffic Safety Administration (NHTSA) revealed that 94% of all traffic accidents are caused by driver error. Of those accidents, 33% could be linked to behaviors typically assigned to road rage, such as illegal maneuvering or misjudging the intent of another driver."[34]

The point is that road rage is very real and something to be aware of. **When confronted with an aggressor the best course of action is to NEVER engage them**. Get out of their way and let them pass by. Don't engage, waive, or even look their way.

If they still won't leave you alone, keep driving and call 9-1-1. They'll tell you what to do and maybe even get help on the way if the situation persists.

Don't assume this can't happen to you if you choose to engage them. For instance, I know someone that was followed home by an aggressive driver who believed they were horribly wronged in that moment and wanted revenge of some sort! Thankfully, the situation didn't get completely out of hand, but it could have. I've known others who have engaged angry drivers as young men. Aside from a lot of yelling, honking, hand gestures, and threats, it never got quite as bad as being followed home, but who knows what could have happened if things escalated.

Understand that people really do act differently on the road from the perceived safety of their vehicles. Perhaps even you will one day too, but there's no reason for things to get that far out of control if you choose not to engage.

Safety Tip # 35: Why You Should Immediately Lock Your Doors Whenever You're in the Car

Keeping your doors locked at all times is something that I want to cover regarding your personal safety because, let's face it, there are bad people out there who may take advantage of you when you're vulnerable, that is, in your vehicle and distracted by your smartphone or the haul from your latest shopping trip. I'm not concerned so much about carjacking situations right now, but more so about times when you're getting in and out of your car, such as in a parking lot.

As a personal example, my niece had a scary moment happen to her a few years ago. To make a long story short, she had just entered her car and, as you might suspect, was preoccupied with her phone before driving off, most likely replying to a text message or on Instagram. Without warning, a person tried to open her passenger door but, because the door was locked, he couldn't get in and immediately hurried off. No doubt she was scared and who's to say what this man wanted. The thing is that she rarely ever locked her doors before then. I'll bet she does now.

Situational awareness is nothing to be overlooked, and it doesn't matter your age or gender. Please keep your awareness about you at all times, particularly when alone.

Semi-Trucks and Large Vehicles Deserve Special Attention

Large vehicles, such as semi-trucks, really do need to be treated differently than other passenger vehicles for a variety of reasons. Let's understand why.

Safety Tip # 36: Braking Distance Matters

Many young people wrongly believe that a semi-truck driver has as much control over their truck as does any passenger vehicle driver. That's simply not true. Semi-trucks are many times larger and heavier than any passenger vehicle which makes them far more difficult to stop.

An acquaintance of mine, Ray, is a part-time semi-truck driver. He says, "You would not believe the things that I see [car] drivers do around big trucks. A loaded semi traveling at 55 mph takes approximately 2 football fields to come to a stop. Also, the brakes on big trucks are air-actuated. There is typically about one-half of a second delay from the time the driver depresses the brake pedal to the time the brakes start to apply. At 60 mph, that's 44 feet of travel."

Realize that two football fields for a semi-truck to stop equals about 600 feet. (FYI, This reference says the stopping distance is closer to 525 feet).[35] When compared to the average stopping distance of a passenger vehicle of just over 300 feet, it's clear that a loaded-down semi-truck just cannot stop as fast as any passenger vehicle can which means you're going to lose in that collision for sure.[36]

Ray goes on to ask: "Is it really worth the risk to try to go in front of a big truck to get off an exit? I've had people slam on the brakes and cut across in front of me to get off the exit that we were about to pass. This happens about twice a month (and I only drive part-time)." Being in a hurry and failing to be aware of your surroundings makes this all too common, I'm afraid. Slow down and exit behind the semi-truck, they'll thank you even if you'll never know it.

Another acquaintance, Frank, concurs: "...an 80,000-pound vehicle traveling 70mph will destroy just about anything Joe Average will be driving. And the one with the most wheels always wins."

Give all large vehicles their due space at all times. This not only includes semi-trucks, but any vehicle much larger than yours. Odds are they can't see what's around them, including you, nearly as well as you can and if they make a mistake you could be the one paying for it, even if they're ultimately at fault.

Safety Tip # 37: Three More Concerns About Large Vehicles and Semi-Trucks to Know

1. If you cannot see the driver in their sideview mirrors, then they cannot see you. This is important for you to fully recognize because, even though most semi-truck drivers are extra cautious, they can't react to something they cannot see. Thus, if you're tailgating them such that they don't know you're there, for instance, you could end up rear-ending them and seriously damaging your vehicle or worse.

2. If you're going to pass a semi-truck, don't waste time. I'm not advocating you speed, but there's no reason to dillydally, especially if the front tires of the truck ever blow out. You could end up crushed underneath the semi-truck before you even know it and then it won't have mattered whatsoever whose fault it was because you'll likely end up permanently injured or dead. Granted, such an accident is a relatively rare occurrence. That said, I would suggest you not willfully drive next to a large truck for an extended period of time.

3. NEVER try to make a turn inside of a turning truck. That is, if there's a semi-truck turning right, but they're in the left-hand lane of two turning lanes, let the truck go first because it may well have to turn into the rightmost lane, which means you're going to get run over. The same can be said for a truck turning left as well. Give them their space.

Getting Your Vehicle Ready for the Road

Being safe on the road isn't only about knowing when it's most dangerous to be driving or even about your habits. It's also about ensuring your vehicle is ready and able to function properly before you get behind the wheel.

After all, realizing that your tires are bald and needed to be replaced AFTER you slide off the road during that first winter storm is the wrong time to find out. Similarly, not having had that sluggish engine looked at before you pulled out into traffic, stalled, and were subsequently T-boned is also the wrong time to find out.

Delaying much-needed vehicle maintenance is a bad decision, and one that could even be deadly.

I won't bore you with all the vehicle maintenance details that most owner's manuals and mechanics would. I will, instead, highlight several areas of concern that you should check on regularly, not only for your safety but for others as well.

Let's understand those now.

Safety Tip # 38: Ensure Your Windshield Is Clean, Inside and Out

You might not realize it, but a dirty windshield can make a huge difference in your ability to see what's ahead of you in the right circumstance. For instance, in that same driver's educational class I watched a video that clearly showed a before and after view of children in a crosswalk who couldn't be seen at all with a slightly dirty windshield because of glaring sunlight that hit at just the right angle. When the windshield was clean, however, the children were easily seen and would surely have been run over as a result. Granted, this scenario was staged, but it did drive home the need for me to keep my windshield relatively clean ever since.

Similarly, the inside of your windshield gets dirty over time as well, but not because of dirt and grime. Instead, the inside gets dirty because of off-gassing from plastics as they age. Cleaning the inside takes some effort and the right supplies but is well worth the time when done right: https://bit.ly/2XhxsHH.[36b] There's no harm in ensuring all other side windows and rear window glass are clean too.

Last, better wiper blades help visibility substantially in the rain and snow. When it's time to replace them go for a mid-priced option as the lesser expensive blades tend not to work as well, in my experience.

Safety Tip # 39: Check Tires Have Adequate Tread and Pressure, and Brakes Function

Tire tread is critical to maintaining proper contact with the road, particularly in rain and snow. If your tires are nearly bald or very worn down, you put yourself at more risk than necessary. Wait long enough and they'll begin to unravel. Here's a quick video on how to check tire tread depth if you don't know how: https://bit.ly/2JPMz2X.[37]

You'll also want to check tire pressure periodically as well because sometimes tires lose a significant amount of air, such as when the weather changes, which could affect your driving safety, especially during poor weather conditions. Checking your tires regularly will also help you know if you have a leak for other reasons like catching a nail, in which case you're going to want to get that fixed ASAP. When inflating tires, follow the manufacturer's recommendations which are usually located on the driver's side door jamb. Remember to inflate the spare tire too.

Similarly, brakes must function properly to be safe as well, though, I'm sure you already know that. Just realize that if your tires squeal constantly then it's time to have them looked at because your brakes may be very worn down indeed and, if you wait long enough, will eventually fail causing a serious scare or worse, not to mention costly repairs to your vehicle.

Safety Tip # 40: Ensure All Fluids Are Topped off Regularly

This includes engine oil, windshield washer fluid, and engine coolant, to name the most likely fluids to be low. Transmission fluid, brake fluid, and power steering fluids are less likely to need added regularly. That said, if any fluids are low (with the exception of windshield washer fluid usage), then there's certainly a problem to be investigated.

Oftentimes dash lights will illuminate to indicate a problem, but not always. If you do have a light come on, though, take your vehicle to a mechanic and find out what the problem is. At the very least, low fluid conditions and leaks should never be ignored.

Honestly, most vehicles can function with far less fluid than required. In fact, I've seen certain family members ignore various low fluid problems over the years and their cars managed to survive. It's not a great idea for your vehicle's longevity, mind you, just not critical to function, with the obvious exception of low brake fluid. That said, there's no reason not to ensure your vehicle's fluids are topped off regularly since it's an easy fix.

Just be safe when checking fluids because some car maintenance tasks, such as checking the coolant level on a hot engine, and even the fluids themselves can seriously injure you if you're not careful.

Safety Tip # 41: Check All Exterior Lights Function

This is something that I feel many people ignore, at least until you get pulled over and are written a ticket. While I understand that sometimes things happen, there's no reason not to take a few minutes every few months to check that your brake lights, headlights, and turn signals function. You may as well check that parking lights and hazards function too.

Safety Tip # 42: Other Maintenance Tasks

There's a wide range of additional routine maintenance that should be considered, including checking the battery, belts, air filters, spark plugs, and more. Most of the above can be easily identified and fixed with routine inspection and maintenance.

If you're unable to do so yourself then have a qualified mechanic perform the inspection and maintenance. In many cases, such as with checking the brakes before imminent failure, you'll save yourself money overall by avoiding costly repairs that didn't need to happen and maybe even save your life.

Last, if your vehicle has any major mechanical concerns, now's the time to have it taken care of because ignoring such problems could leave you stranded one day.

Safety Tip # 43: Be Able to Jump-Start Your Own Car and Change a Flat Tire

The two most likely reasons you'll wind up stranded are a dead battery and a flat tire. A good set of jumper cables, therefore, are an obvious addition.[38] I would also suggest a 12-volt DC tire pump for times when you only need a bit of air to make it to the nearest gas station or mechanic after picking up a nail that caused a slow leak.[38b]

In addition, I would encourage you to get a vehicle jump-starter power bank because you cannot always count on another driver coming by to help you out in a timely manner.[39] Plus, you never know if someone with bad intentions might show up, and having the ability get yourself back on the road quickly is wonderful.

If you're unaware, a jump-starter power bank is basically a large lithium battery powerful enough to jump start a car battery once. Know that there are different peak amperage ratings depending on the vehicle you drive, which means you'll want to match the power bank to your vehicle's battery capacity.

You should also (1) ensure that your spare tire is aired up occasionally because they often aren't after years of neglect and (2) have the appropriate tools to change a tire. If you don't know how to safely change a tire, watch this video: https://bit.ly/2UUYbYS.[40]

Safety Tip # 44: Get AAA or Sign up for Your Insurance Company's Alternative

Sometimes you have bigger car problems than you can solve on your own, or you just don't want to get dirty changing a tire. I get it. For a reasonable monthly or yearly fee, services such as AAA or your insurance company's version may pay for itself the first time you ever need it.[41]

Often, they'll perform services such as jump-starting the battery or changing a tire, unlocking your car, filling it with gas, and will even tow you to a mechanic should it come to that.

Personally, we've had AAA for years and have used it more than a few times with our ever-aging vehicles. These days we wouldn't be without it.

Alternatively, you may be able to save a few dollars over AAA by going with your insurance company's plan which, unfortunately, usually isn't included in your premiums and, from what I've researched myself, tends to be severely limited in the services offered.

Do your research and I'm sure you'll find a good option that fits your budget and needs, and don't assume you'll never need help because you will at some point.

Safety Tip # 45: Be Able to Charge Your Phone and Include Numbers to Call for Help

Because a phone is your sole lifeline to get help when out driving on your own, it's important to always ensure your phone is functioning properly, and keeping the battery charged is crucial to that end. Fortunately, there are a few ways to do so.

For starters, get an auxiliary DC charger and appropriate cord for your phone. That way you should be able to use the vehicle's battery to charge your phone unless the car battery has died. Aftermarket cord alternatives can often be found online for only a few dollars and usually work well enough.

If you get the aforementioned jump-starter power bank, then they almost always have USB ports for charging phones and other electronics. Moreover, there are a wide variety of portable power packs which are similar to the vehicle jump-starter power bank, only much smaller, available online as well that work great for this purpose.[42]

Last, be sure to have appropriate phone numbers you may need to call for help already programmed into your phone. This could be AAA as mentioned previously, a family friend, or a trusted neighbor. Just be sure you clearly know who to contact and that your phone will be functional when needed.

Safety Tip # 46: Some Final Thoughts on Getting Your Vehicle Ready for the Road

It never hurts to keep your gas tank half full or more in case you get stuck in traffic. I would also have a few extra supplies in your car so that you're ready for the unexpected. Besides the aforementioned items, like tools to change a flat tire or the jump-starter power bank, you may want to include road flares, gloves, a safety vest, and a flashlight, at minimum. If you live anywhere that it tends to snow, then you might also want snow chains for better traction and a small shovel to dig your way out if you get stuck.

I would also encourage you to keep some shelf-stable snacks and a few water bottles in the trunk. You're going to want to swap these foodstuffs out periodically, say, twice a year because they will tend to go bad much faster than normal when exposed to temperature extremes. And if you choose to consume them for whatever reason then be sure to replace what was taken as soon as possible.

Also, it couldn't hurt to include an old jacket, socks, sneakers, stocking cap, and even a blanket as well, just in case you get stranded or must walk to safety.

Personally, I keep many more items in my vehicle because I like to be prepared for a variety of scenarios, but these items are the basics that everyone should have.

Sobering Statistics for Teen Drivers

As much as new, teen driver's want their freedom—and as much as we parents want them to have it—the statistics for teen driver casualties really must be reiterated. According to this NHTSA article, adapted to fit here:

- In 2016, there were 2,082 teen drivers of passenger vehicles involved in fatal motor vehicle traffic crashes.
- In 2016, 58 percent of all passenger fatalities of 15- to 18-year-old passenger vehicle drivers were unrestrained.
- In 2016, almost 20 percent of the teen drivers involved in fatal crashes were drinking.
- In 2016, 10 percent of fatal crashes involving a teen driver, the teen driver was distracted at the time of the crash.
- In 2016, there were 2,288 motor vehicle traffic fatalities in crashes that involved passenger vehicles [driven by] teen drivers aged 15 to 18 years old.[43]

I'm sure you're getting tired of statistics by now, but they really do tell the same story over and over again: teenagers are more at risk for fatal car accidents because of poor decision making above all else.

Safety Tips # 47-49: The Biggest Risk Factors and What to do About Them

The same NHTSA article goes on to state that: "Teen drivers are involved in vehicle crashes not because they are uninformed about the basic rules of the road or safe driving practices; rather, studies show teens are involved in crashes because of inexperience and risk-taking. Teen drivers, particularly 16- and 17-year-olds, have high fatal crash rates because of their immaturity and limited driving experience, which often result in high-risk behavior behind the wheel. Peer pressure is an especially potent factor. In a recent NHTSA study, teens were two-and-a-half times more likely to engage in potentially risky behavior when driving with a teenage peer versus driving alone. The likelihood increased to three times when traveling with multiple passengers."[43]

Let me reiterate two points regarding accidents and teens, specifically that teen drivers are more likely to engage in high-risk driving behaviors because:

1. They're inexperienced, and
2. Peer pressure from friends

Parents can dramatically affect both behaviors by (1) getting you behind the wheel as much as possible during your learner's permit period and (2) not allowing you to drive friends at all until you're much older, let's say, thirty? Ok, eighteen-years-old it is.

How to Drive Safely Recap

I do hope that most of this is common sense or, at the very least, an eye-opening, yet sobering look at being safe on the road. Sadly, teen drivers are the most at-risk group for fatal accidents, in large part, due to their inexperience and peer pressure.

Ultimately, being safe on the road boils down to not putting yourself at risk for accidents. This includes avoiding or reducing risky behavior, such as speeding, driving while intoxicated, texting while driving, running lights because you're in a hurry, and giving into peer pressure, to name a handful of the more important ones.

Being safe also means consciously doing things to increase your odds of survival or to reduce the odds of an accident, including wearing your seat belt, turning on headlights for safety, or just plain ensuring your vehicle functions correctly.

And, though we've pointed out days and times when we're most at risk while on the road, please don't assume that other days or times are inherently safe. Accidents happen all the time and can happen without you even having the time to react. You simply must be vigilant each time you get behind the wheel.

I do want to make one more point here: I can't help but notice crosses next to roadways, the ones that indicate a loved-one died there from a car accident. I invariably wonder what happened, whether a teenager was involved, and if it could have been prevented. Odds are that it could have been knowing what we know now, which brings up another very important point...

Most of these fatal accidents—and most accidents, in general—are clearly preventable by slowing down, paying attention to what's going on, and using a bit of common sense.

Drill this information into your head as much as you can. I'm not saying that you should read it over and over again, but you can certainly spend a few minutes talking to your parents about what you've read within by using the accompanying checklist and continue to think about safe driving habits as you progress through your learner's permit period.

I figure the more you hear and read this information the more likely it will be to sink in. Print off the checklist and post it somewhere that you might glance at it occasionally.

Get Your Free Checklist Here

Before you grab your checklist, be a good friend or family member and choose to help others who could use this crucial information for their new teenager driver's as well...

Spread the Word, Share the Knowledge

I'm willing to bet that you have family and friends who could benefit from this book as well, so please take a moment right now and quickly share a link to it on Facebook, Twitter, or Pinterest. You can easily do so here.[44]

If you haven't done so yet, download your free, easy-to-reference checklist here.[45] Or, the entire checklist is reproduced in Appendix A.

Discover More Books Here

If you liked what you read within then you're going to love my other books.[46] Here's a sampling:

- 53 Essential Bug Out Bag Supplies[47]
- 47 Easy DIY Survival Projects[48]
- The Complete Pet Safety Action Plan[49]
- 28 Powerful Home Security Solutions[50]
- 27 Crucial Smartphone Apps for Survival[51]
- 57 Scientifically-Proven Survival Foods to Stockpile[52]
- 75 of the Best Secret Hiding Places[53]
- Your Identity Theft Protection Game Plan[54]
- 144 Survival Uses for 10 Common Items[55]

And if you would like to be among the first to know when new books become available, fill out this form and you'll be notified via email.[56]

Your Opinion Matters to Me

I'd love to hear your feedback about this book, especially anything I might be able to add or improve upon for future revisions. Please send an email to rethinksurvival@gmail.com with the word "book" in the subject if you have something for me. (And be sure to include the book title so I'm not confused.)

Review This Book on Amazon

Last, I ask that you take a moment and write a review of my book on Amazon.com so that others know what to expect, particularly if you've found my advice useful.[57]

I do hope that you've enjoyed this book and that you will choose to heed my recommendations so that you, as a new, teenage driver stay safe on the road.

I encourage you to please take a moment and download the checklist above, share this book with your friends and family as you see fit, and leave a quick review on Amazon.com while you're at it.

May God bless you and your family.

Thank you for your time, Damian

List of Figures

Figure 1

Title, Description: Aftermath of Storm Sandy (hit Arlington on October 29th, 2012).
Author: Arlington County (https://www.flickr.com/people/38511994@N07).
Image Source:
https://commons.wikimedia.org/wiki/File:Storm_Downed_power_lines_and_trees_from_Storm_Sandy_(8138919297).jpg[58]
License: Creative Commons Attribution-Share Alike 2.0 Generic license (https://creativecommons.org/licenses/by-sa/2.0/deed.en).
Modifications: No changes were made to this image.

Figure 2

Title, Description: Moggill Road looking outbound from Manyung Street at Moggill Creek Bridge in the Brisbane suburb of Kenmore.
Author: Rob Webb, Kenmore, Brisbane, QLD.
Image Source:
https://commons.wikimedia.org/wiki/File:Moggill_Road_outbound_at_Moggill_Creek_Bridge_flooded_in_the_Brisbane_suburb_of_Kenmore_2011.JPG[59]
License: Creative Commons Attribution-Share Alike 3.0 Unported license (https://creativecommons.org/licenses/by-

sa/3.0/deed.en).
Modifications: No changes were made to this image.

Figure 3

Title, Description: Sunlight Piercing Through Green
Tall Trees during Daytime.
Author: pixabay.com.
Image Source:
https://www.pexels.com/photo/sunlight-piercing-
through-green-tall-trees-during-daytime-47864/[60]
License: Creative Commons Zero (CC0) license
(https://www.pexels.com/photo-license/).
Modifications: No changes were made to this image.

Figure 4

Title, Description: Don't text and drive.
Author: Kelly White.
Image Source:
http://www.tinker.af.mil/News/Photos/igphoto/200
0839089/[61]
License: Found using Google Image Search with
"Usage Rights: Labeled for reuse with modification."
Modifications: No changes were made to this image.

Figure 5

Title, Description: A hairpin turn at the east end of
Dongshan Road, Sec. 2, Taichung City, Taiwan.
Author: Yoxem
(https://commons.wikimedia.org/wiki/User_talk:Yox

em).
Image Source:
https://commons.wikimedia.org/wiki/File:Hairpin_T
urn_of_Dongshan_Road,_Sec._2.JPG[62]
License: Creative Commons Attribution 3.0 Unported
license(https://creativecommons.org/licenses/by/3.
0/deed.en).
Modifications: No changes were made to this image.

Appendices

Appendix A: 49-Point Checklist

Appendix B: List of Resources

Appendix A: 49-Point Checklist

The Statistics

- Research has found that dialing a phone number while driving increases your teen's risk of crashing by six times, and texting while driving increases the risk by 23 times...in 52 percent of all wrecks, drivers had been on their phones. These aren't just fender benders – 29 percent of drivers were doing over 56 miles per hour.

- For drivers involved in fatal crashes, young males are the most likely to be speeding... In 2012, 24 percent of female drivers in the 15- to 20-year-old age group and 19 percent of female drivers in the 21- to 24-year-old age group involved in fatal crashes were speeding at the time of the crash. Among males, 37 percent of 15- to 20-year-old and 37 percent of 21- to 24-year-old drivers involved in fatal crashes were speeding.

- Age is a huge factor in who gets ticketed... Those in the 16 – 25-year-old demographic got one third of all speeding tickets in the study. While drivers 40 and over got another third, the two groups are very different in size. The younger group makes up less than 15 percent of the state's population while the older group is just about half the state... When graphed by age, there is a huge decline in tickets after the age of 19. And this holds true for both male and female drivers.

- Deaths caused by red light running are increasing at more than three times the rate of increase for all other fatal crashes. More people are injured in crashes involving red light running than in any other crash type.
- Car accident statistics are jarring at night. Despite 60 percent less traffic on the roads, more than 40 percent of all fatal car accidents occur at night.
- 80% of drivers admit to having some type of road rage during the course of a year... [and] at least 8 million drivers engage in some type of road rage each year.
- More recent data from the National Highway Traffic Safety Administration (NHTSA) revealed that 94% of all traffic accidents are caused by driver error. Of those accidents, 33% could be linked to behaviors typically assigned to road rage, such as illegal maneuvering or misjudging the intent of another driver.
- In a recent NHTSA study, teens were two-and-a-half times more likely to engage in potentially risky behavior when driving with a teenage peer versus driving alone. The likelihood increased to three times when traveling with multiple passengers.
- In 2012, 28 percent of the speeding drivers under age 21 who were involved in fatal crashes also had BACs of .08 g/dL or higher [more than double non-speeding drivers]... For drivers 21 to 24 years old

who were involved in fatal crashes in 2012, 50 percent of speeding drivers had BACs of .08 g/dL or higher, compared with only 24 percent of non-speeding drivers.

- Fender-benders are 14% more likely to happen on the first day of snow than later in the snowy season... [and] SUVs make up about 16% of all crashes. But consistently, when winter arrives, that percentage moves up to 18%.

- The Centers for Disease Control and Prevention report that over half of all flood-related drownings occur when a vehicle is driven into hazardous flood water. The next highest percentage of flood-related deaths is due to walking into or near flood waters.

The Most Dangerous Driving Times, Days, and Situations

1. Most dangerous time of the day are weekdays between 3 pm to 7 pm (rush hour after work or school) and after midnight on Friday night.
2. Dusk and dawn driving can be dangerous as well due to drowsiness, shadows, sunlight angle, as well as other driver's not turning on their headlights.
3. Most dangerous days to drive for teens are the 100 deadliest days from Memorial Day through Labor Day (the summer months), with emphasis on weekends in August. Major holiday weekends

are dangerous for all of us as well, including July 4th, Christmas, New Year's, Memorial Day, etc.

4. The first day of snowstorms are worse than all others combined.

5. SUVs aren't any safer in inclement weather (with regards to braking and turning) than any other vehicle and, in fact, may be more dangerous to drive due to the perception of being safer.

6. Any inclement weather can be dangerous, including heavy rains (which can result in hydroplaning), dense fog, glaring sunlight, high winds, etc.

7. Never drive over downed power lines as they can still be energized and, therefore, fatal to touch, even in the perceived safety of a vehicle.

8. Never driver over flooded roads either. A mere 12 inches of rushing water is enough to sweep a car down the road and is the most likely reason for flood-related drownings.

Always Do This Before Driving Off

9. Ensure the driver's seat, steering wheel, mirrors, and headrest are positioned correctly. Get everything else situated as well (e.g., music, GPS directions, A/C or heater).

10. Hold steering wheel at 9 and 3 instead of 10 and 2 for airbag deployment safety.

11. Always wear seat belts. The statistics are undeniable that seat belts save lives.

12. Turn your headlights on for safety, even during the day.

Not Speeding is Much More Than Avoiding Speeding Tickets

13. Speeding is a major factor in traffic accidents with young age and alcohol use being the two biggest contributing factors for young drivers.
14. Speeding doesn't save time in most driving scenarios, especially city driving and shorter distances of less than an hour.
15. Teens are far more likely to be targeted for speeding than all other age groups.
16. Even a few miles per hour change in speed makes a huge difference in preventing accidents due to reaction times and braking distances.
17. Use the 3-second trick for preventing car accidents at any speed.

Don't Do Any of This While Driving

18. Avoid distractions while driving, including eating, applying makeup, and, most importantly, NEVER texting or using the smartphone while driving. It's the #1 distraction for teen drivers.
19. Don't wear earbuds or headsets while driving or, at the very least, never cover both ears.
20. Don't follow other vehicles too closely, especially at highway speeds. Allow 10 feet of distance for

every 10 miles per hour in speed at minimum. Add more for inclement weather.

21. Stop trying to make yellow and red lights. Running red lights dramatically increases the chances for side-impact collisions and running yellows means you're probably speeding to do so.

22. Railroad crossings are fatal too! Never try to beat the train... it will always win.

Communicate with Other Drivers Properly and Respectfully

23. Communicate with other drivers by using your blinkers to signal turns and lane changes.

24. Use brake lights to signal slow-downs, hazards when stopped unexpectedly on the road.

25. Use your high beam lights appropriately, never in the fog, and to signal oncoming drivers only if necessary.

26. Use your horn to avoid collisions; never to get others to speed up, move out of the way, etc.

More Commonsense Safety Tips to Know

27. Give yourself 5 or 10 extra minutes to get where you're going. In so doing, you won't be rushed and will be less likely to make a hasty decision or to speed unnecessarily.

28. Pedestrians always get the right of way at intersections and crosswalks; give them plenty of

leeway in parking lots too. The same goes for cyclists and motorcyclists.

29. If you're feeling tired, pull over to rest or call somebody to come get you.

30. Medications and drug interactions may cause drowsiness. Ensure any new medications don't adversely affect your mental awareness before getting behind the wheel.

31. Avoid late night driving, if possible. Driving at night increases your risk for being in an accident about threefold alone.

32. Road signs and street markings really are trying to help you stay safe. Pay attention to them as there are often multiple indicators of wrong behavior. Sold-yellow lines, too, are not optional to ignore when passing slower vehicles. Blind corners, dips and rises over hills cannot be seen beyond properly and, therefore, shouldn't be risked.

33. Move over for emergency and stopped vehicles always. They're either in a hurry to get somewhere or will appreciate the extra space.

34. Road rage is real and more prevalent than most realize. Never engage them and call 9-1-1 if the aggressive behavior towards you continues.

35. Lock your doors whenever you're in the vehicle, such as sitting in a parking lot at night, for your personal safety.

Semi-Trucks and Large Vehicles Deserve Special Attention

36. Give semi-trucks and other large vehicles plenty of warning time and space to slow down; a fully-loaded semi-truck needs about twice the stopping distance of a typical passenger car.
37. A few more concerns about large vehicle and semi-trucks:
    a. If you cannot see the driver in their sideview mirrors, they cannot see you.
    b. Don't waste time passing up a semi-truck in order to avoid tire blowouts, but don't speed to do so either. And don't drive next to a large truck for an extended period of time either.
    c. NEVER try to make a turn inside of a turning semi-truck, you may get run over and be at fault or, worse, cause a fatal accident.

Getting Your Vehicle Ready for the Road

38. Ensure your windshield in clean, inside and out. You'd be surprised at what you cannot see when it's dirty!
39. Check that tires have adequate tread and pressure, and that brakes function.
40. Ensure all fluids are topped off regularly and that you know how to check them properly and safely.
41. Check that all exterior lights function (e.g., brake lights, headlights, turn signals).

42. Other maintenance tasks: check battery, belts, filters, spark plugs, etc.
43. Have the ability to jump-start your own car (with a power pack) and to change a flat tire.
44. Get AAA or sign up for your insurance company's alternative to deal with bigger problems.
45. Have the ability to charge your phone so that you can call for help if needed and program phone numbers they would need to call for help.
46. Keep your gas tank half full, and include additional safety items in your car, such as road flares, gloves, a safety vest, flashlight, small shovel, snow chains, food, water, extra clothes, shoes, and blanket.

Biggest Risk Factors for New, Teen Drivers

47. Their inexperience driving (which causes them to make hasty, poor decisions).
48. Peer pressure from friends (which causes them to make dumb, even reckless decisions).
49. Get them as much driving time behind the wheel as you can during their learner's permit months. And, even if your state allows the behavior, keep their friends out of the car for the first year or two of their driving careers.

Appendix B: List of Resources

- Link 1: https://rethinksurvival.com/books/safe-driving-checklist.php
- Link 2: https://rethinksurvival.com/books/safe-driving-book-offer.php
- Link 3: https://rethinksurvival.com/kindle-books/
- Link 4: http://www.clinardinsurance.com/contact/faqs/355-what-is-the-most-dangerous-time-of-day-for-teen-drivers
- Link 5: https://bottomlineinc.com/life/driving/dusk-dawn-driving-can-deadly
- Link 6: https://www.snopes.com/holidays/newyears/traffic.asp
- Link 7: https://www.cbsnews.com/news/memorial-day-driving-car-accidents/
- Link 8: https://driversed.com/trending/most-dangerous-times-for-driving
- Link 9: http://minnesota.cbslocal.com/2011/01/31/good-question-safer-in-winter-cars-or-suvs/
- Link 10: https://www.youtube.com/watch?v=spaOeDD3rgo

- Link 11:
  https://www.pge.com/en_US/safety/electrical-safety/what-to-do-if-you-see-a-downed-power-line/what-to-do-if-you-see-a-downed-power-line.page
- Link 12:
  https://www.indianaec.org/2015/01/30/protect-learning-four-common-myths-power-lines/
- Link 13: https://www.weather.gov/safety/flood-turn-around-dont-drown
- Link 13b:
  https://www.youtube.com/watch?v=kkQX2gkwJoE
- Link 14:
  https://www.seattlepi.com/local/transportation/article/10-and-2-no-longer-safe-way-to-hold-steering-3453234.php
- Link 15:
  https://www.cdc.gov/motorvehiclesafety/seatbelts/facts.html
- Link 16:
  https://www.youtube.com/watch?v=YLCWGcNpY94
- Link 17:
  https://www.youtube.com/watch?v=d7iYZPp2zYY
- Link 18:
  https://www.youtube.com/watch?v=PRH5rYUHoVU

- Link 19: http://drivinglaws.aaa.com/tag/headlight-use/
- Link 20: http://www.dot.state.mn.us/research/TRS/2011/TRS1009.pdf
- Link 21: https://crashstats.nhtsa.dot.gov/Api/Public/View Publication/812021
- Link 22: https://lifehacker.com/does-speeding-really-get-you-there-any-faster-1556767685
- Link 23: https://www.roadandtrack.com/car-culture/a12042701/who-gets-speeding-tickets-and-why/
- Link 24: https://seriousaccidents.com/legal-advice/top-causes-of-car-accidents/speeding/
- Link 25: https://www.nhtsa.gov/road-safety/teen-driving
- Link 26: https://www.aol.com/article/news/2017/04/04/study-majority-of-car-accidents-caused-by-distracted-driving/22024897/
- Link 26b: Link 26b: https://onmyway.com/
- Link 27: http://drivinglaws.aaa.com/tag/headsets/
- Link 28: https://www.clevelandtexas.com/DocumentCenter/View/113/Red-Light-Running-Facts-PDF
- Link 29: https://oli.org/about-us/news/collisions-casulties

- Link 29b: https://www.youtube.com/watch?v=GduFDV_oY2s
- Link 30: http://drivinginstructorblog.com/q-illegal-turn-signal/
- Link 31: https://www.fda.gov/Drugs/ResourcesForYou/ucm079514.htm
- Link 32: https://seriousaccidents.com/legal-advice/top-causes-of-car-accidents/nighttime-driving/
- Link 33: https://www.creditdonkey.com/road-rage-statistics.html
- Link 34: http://drivingschool.net/road-rage-statistics-filled-surprising-facts/
- Link 35: https://www.hg.org/legal-articles/stopping-distances-for-commercial-vehicles-28265
- Link 36: https://nacto.org/docs/usdg/vehicle_stopping_distance_and_time_upenn.pdf
- Link 36b: https://www.youtube.com/watch?v=axI5Luw0Eos
- Link 37: https://www.youtube.com/watch?v=TvK2_2hGygw
- Link 38: https://rethinksurvival.com/kindle-books/safe-driving-recommends#jumpercables

- Link 38b: https://rethinksurvival.com/kindle-books/safe-driving-recommends#tirepump
- Link 39: https://rethinksurvival.com/kindle-books/safe-driving-recommends#powerbank
- Link 40: https://www.youtube.com/watch?v=joBmbh0AGSQ
- Link 41: https://aaa.com/
- Link 42: https://rethinksurvival.com/kindle-books/safe-driving-recommends#powerpack
- Link 43: https://www.nhtsa.gov/road-safety/teen-driving
- Link 44: https://rethinksurvival.com/books/safe-driving-share.html
- Link 45: https://rethinksurvival.com/books/safe-driving-checklist.php
- Link 46: https://rethinksurvival.com/kindle-books/
- Link 47: https://rethinksurvival.com/kindle-books/bug-out-bag-book/
- Link 48: https://rethinksurvival.com/kindle-books/diy-survival-projects-book/
- Link 49: https://rethinksurvival.com/kindle-books/pet-safety-plan-book/
- Link 50: https://rethinksurvival.com/kindle-books/home-security-book/
- Link 51: https://rethinksurvival.com/kindle-books/smartphone-survival-apps-book/

- Link 52: https://rethinksurvival.com/kindle-books/survival-foods-book/
- Link 53: https://rethinksurvival.com/kindle-books/secret-hides-book/
- Link 54: https://rethinksurvival.com/kindle-books/id-theft-book/
- Link 55: https://rethinksurvival.com/kindle-books/survival-uses-book/
- Link 56: https://rethinksurvival.com/books/new-survival-books.php
- Link 57: https://rethinksurvival.com/books/safe-driving-review.php
- Link 58: https://commons.wikimedia.org/wiki/File:Storm_Downed_power_lines_and_trees_from_Storm_Sandy_(8138919297).jpg
- Link 59: https://commons.wikimedia.org/wiki/File:Moggil_Road_outbound_at_Moggill_Creek_Bridge_flooded_in_the_Brisbane_suburb_of_Kenmore_2011.JPG
- Link 60: https://www.pexels.com/photo/sunlight-piercing-through-green-tall-trees-during-daytime-47864/
- Link 61: http://www.tinker.af.mil/News/Photos/igphoto/2000839089/

- Link 62:
  https://commons.wikimedia.org/wiki/File:Hairpi
  n_Turn_of_Dongshan_Road,_Sec._2.JPG

Made in the USA
Monee, IL
17 October 2020